The Moon and the Whippoorwill

By Michael Gillespie

Illustrations by Britt Harrison
and Michael Gillespie

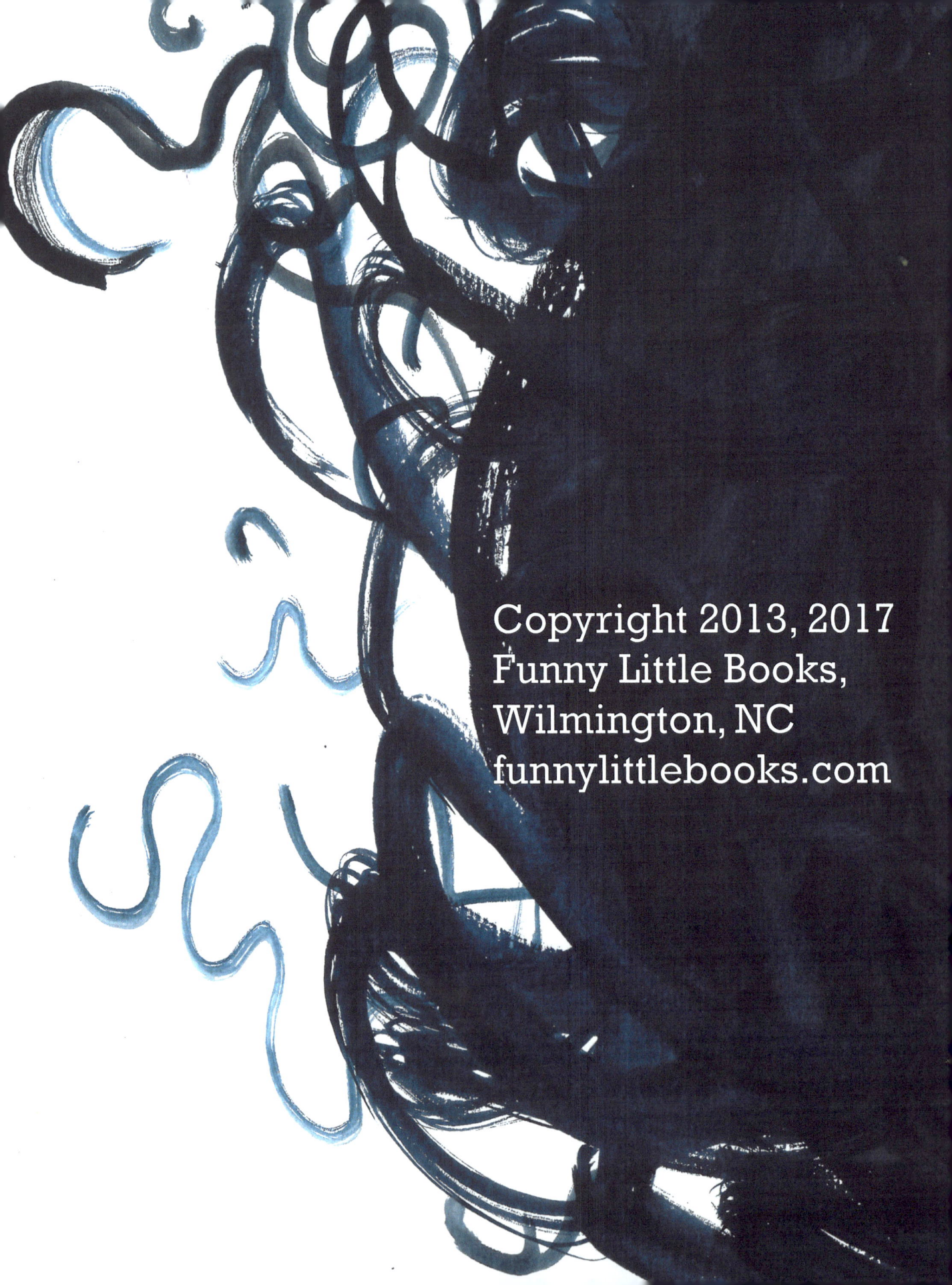

Dedicated to
Full Moons, Tears, and Dreams,
Bright, pure, and real.
You inspire us all to sing,
To live, and to feel.

The Whippoorwill loved the Moon
More than he loved anything else,
As much as most people care
For the things they care for most,

As much
as a puppy loves a child,
as a kitten loves a butterfly,
as a friend loves a friend,
and as the sun loves the rain.

With every mile
That he flew
And with every note
That he sang,
The Whippoorwill
loved the Moon.

One night
The Whippoorwill looked to the Moon,
And she was smaller by far,
A thin slice of the fair beauty
who had shown down before.

He knew in his heart
His moon would depart,
and he felt in his breast
something a song could tell best.

Oh, my Moon, he sang,
I will never let you go!

With every song from my bill,
Every high whip, low poor, and high will
I will call to you,
and you will stay.

I will not believe,
that you would ever leave.
I would rather sing,
with my eyes closed,
For the rest of my days
Than know sorrows
like this.

That is not true,
said the Moon,
On a breeze through the trees
that trembled the leaves

Good bye, Moon,
said the Whippoorwill,

Fine, I will not keep my eyes closed,
but what good will it do?

You are my only companion,
My nighttime companion,
My heavenly lantern.
You head west
to the sea
leaving me
lonely
and alone.

That is not true,
said the Moon,
On a breeze through the trees
that trembled the leaves

Good bye, Moon,
said the Whippoorwill,

Yes, okay, there are birds of a feather,
happily chirping and flocking together,
but they are not you!

Why Love? Why do you leave?
The song that I sang was in one key,
Yours,
Every moment was a gift,
This will cut me adrift,

You must hate me.

That is not true,
said the Moon,
On a breeze through the trees
that trembled the leaves

Good bye, Moon, said the Whippoorwill,

But wait!! I could leave all this,
Maybe it would be best
If I took to wing and
followed you west
I may be no spring chicken
but I have fire in my chest,
Without you, I have nothing,
just a twiggy nest.

Where there's
a whippoorwill
there's a way,
The great western ocean
is not
too
wide to find
You.

That is not true,
said the Moon,
On a breeze through the trees
that trembled the leaves

Good bye, Moon, said the Whippoorwill,

The shadow I cast,
I swear, with you gone,
the shadow will be less
down the paths that we wandered,
In the field, on the long grass.

It will be as if
The world has gone dim.

That is not true,
said the Moon,
On a breeze through the trees
that trembled the leaves

The Whippoorwill looked to the sky,
The night was half over,
His Moon, half way down
Her path through the heavens.

His chest
filled with a sigh.
Tears
swelled in his eyes.

Down his beak,
Against his cheek,
He felt the breath
of the moon.

Good bye Moon, said the Whippoorwill,

I will miss
the kiss of you gaze
The pure white light that was lighting
the nights of my days.

On the tips of my wings,
and in my memories I will know
and remember
the smallest,
softest,
sweetest of things,
Your glow.

That
is worth missing.

That is true,
said the Moon,
On a breeze through the trees
barely lifting the leaves.

Good bye, Moon, said the Whippoorwill,

I will remember
Your tresses,
The long flowing moonbeams of
Your purest essence.
On the world like an echo,
Your clean light lingers.

We shared
something special.

That is true,
said the Moon,
On a breeze through the trees
barely lifting the leaves.

Good bye, Moon, said the Whippoorwill,

It is not
As hopeless as it seems,
You cradled me always
In flight and in dreams.
You filled up with love
My little Whippoorwill heart
So much that the love expanded
And tore boundaries apart.

And now I hold you dear
And whole in my breast,
Light for my life,
Only the best,

And
I know
That you carry west
a part of me too.

That is true,
said the Moon,
On a breeze through the trees
barely lifting the leaves.

Good bye, Moon, said the Whippoorwill

You gave me courage,
You taught me to fly,
And when the limbs of the woods
Nearly blocked the sky
You would shine a little light,
I might never know why.

You bathed me
In moon beams,
You lit me on fire,
Now I will sing,
For I know, that is
What you would desire.

That is true,
said the Moon,
On a breeze through the trees
barely lifting the leaves.

As he curled down in his nest,
the Whippoorwill sang,

Goodbye, Moon,

I will never forget you

I love you

I will fly the paths you have shown me

And I will sing

Whip – poor – will

and the Moon echoed,

Good bye, said the Moon.

I will never forget you, said the Moon.

Love more, and more often, said the Moon.

Fly higher, find new paths, said the Moon.

Sing for us all, said the Moon.

Whip – poor – will,
   echoed the Moon,
      Whip – poor – will.
         On a breeze through the trees
         barely lifting the leaves,
           Whip – poor – will.

The Cast

Whippoorwill Bill,
who sings nocturnal themes.
His Moon,
who echoes cool dreams.

Another little creature
appearing upbidden
in a bit part
but otherwise un-bitten,
Mr. Baseball, a shy little bat.

Thank you for reading this little book. I truly hope it resonates with you and makes your day or night slightly better. I would enjoy hearing if you liked it!

Your Author,
Michael
funnylittlebooks.com

Britt Harrison, Painter, Illustrator, Artist

Britt Harrison uses painting, sculpture and printmaking to address concepts about our existential curiosities and our need to control the natural and unnatural world around us. Drawing visual inspiration from moments of her remote upbringing in Southern America, she uses imagery of animals and nature to critique human interaction and the significance of connection and honesty.

Britt Harrison was born in Winston-Salem, North Carolina and studied art theory, studio art and psychology at New York University and the University of North Carolina at Wilmington. She is the Co-Founder, Co-Creative Director, and Writer at Future Tongue, an artist collective that explores the contemporary art culture of Los Angeles through studio visits and interviews.

www.brittharrison.com

https://www.funnylittlebooks.com/brittharrison/

Michael Gillespie, Author, and little creature Illustrator

Michael Gillespie grew up in a house full of books and surrounded by woods. He lives in Wilmington, NC and practices law. In 2011, after receiving pictures from his Aunt Mary and Uncle Gray of baby owls living in their backyard, he wrote his first children's story, Whose Hoo?. Other little stories include The Moon and the Whippoorwill (2017), The Unremarkable Little Thing, Jazz Moles , The Fox and the Sloth: Let's Go Big! (expected late 2017), and Game of Cones (expected early 2018).

https://www.FunnyLittleBooks.com/MichaelGillespie

www.ingramcontent.com/pod-product-compliance
Lightning Source LLC
Chambersburg PA
CBHW042102040426
42448CB00002B/112